D0429091

DISCARDED

Growing into Love

Books by X. J. Kennedy

GROWING INTO LOVE

NUDE DESCENDING A STAIRCASE

GROWING
INTO
LOVE

by X. J. Kennedy, 1929–

PS
3521
E563
G7

811
K 36

Doubleday & Company, Inc.
Garden City, New York

For Dorothy
at last, as all along

Acknowledgments

Some of these poems, as they are now or in earlier versions, first appeared in the following publications: *Agenda, Open Places, Carolina Quarterly, The American Scholar, The Atlantic, The Brown Bag, Chelsea, West Coast Review, New Statesman, Paris Review, Southern Poetry Review, Transatlantic Review, Can. The New Yorker, Golgotha* and *O'Riley's Late-bloomed Little Son; Sou'wester, Wish* and *Main Road West,* Copyright © 1968 by The Board of Trustees of Southern Illinois University; *Burning Deck, Birth Report* and *Hearthside Story,* Copyright © 1965 by Burning Deck; *Commonweal, The Shorter View,* Copyright © 1969 by Commonweal Publishing Co., Inc.; *Kayak, The Nineteen-thirties,* Copyright © 1967 by George Hitchcock, Publisher, Kayak; *Poetry, National Shrine, Peace and Plenty, Ant Trap,* Copyright © 1969 by Modern Poetry Association; *Poetry Northwest, Absentminded Bartender,* Apocrypha, *Mean Gnome Day,* Copyright © 1967 by Poetry Northwest; *Of Poetry and Power: Poems Occasioned by the Presidency and by the Death of John F. Kennedy,* edited by Erwin A. Glikes and Paul Schwaber (Basic Books, Inc.), *Down in Dallas; First Prospectus for an Oberlin Quarterly, Nothing in Heaven Functions as It Ought,* and *Artificer,* Copyright 1962 by the Yeoman Committee for an Oberlin Quarterly; *The Other End of the Couch: Poems for Gordon Cairnie* (The Carthage Press); *A Controversy of Poets* (Anchor Books).

The poem *Ant Trap* makes a reference to the poem by Winfield Townley Scott, *The U. S. Sailor with the Japanese Skull.*

I should like to thank Andrew Robert Longyear for contributing the rime "pewter/computer," and the National Council on the Arts and the Humanities and the Trustees of Tufts College for free time to complete this collection.

X.J.K.

Contents

I. Experiences

II. Countrymen

III. Growing into Love

I
Experiences

Cross Ties

Out walking ties left over from a track
Where nothing travels now but rust and grass,
I could take stock in something that would pass
Bearing down Hell-bent from behind my back:
A thing to sidestep or go down before,
Far-off, indifferent as that curfew's wail
The evening wind flings like a sack of mail
Or close up as the moon whose headbeam stirs
A flock of cloud to make tracks. Down to strafe
The bristled grass a hawk falls—there's a screech
Like steel wrenched taut till severed. Out of reach
Or else beneath desiring, I go safe,
Walk on, tensed for a leap, unreconciled
To a dark void all kindness.
                                    When I spill
The salt I throw the Devil some and, still,
I let them sprinkle water on my child.

Snapshots

I

BIRTH REPORT

When blam! my father's gun began the dash
Of fifty thousand tadpoles for one egg,
I set myself without a leg to leg
Like sixty for the tape. A tungsten flash,
And then my mother in a nest my aunt
Had paid for let me down.
                          How can so short
A time have worn so dim the birth report
White, Anglo-Saxon, one-half Protestant?

II

When Wall Street swallowed brokers whole
And dust clouds chased their tails like dogs,
I was afforded baby togs,
Mouth outstretched like a beggar's bowl.
Not knowing who'd been let to live
Or who'd been herded in and gassed,
I slept. The sky's bough broke. Down fell
The Hindenburg's big blue hornet's nest.

Poets

These people are . . . quenched. I mean the natives.

*D. H. Lawrence, letter of 14 August 1923
from Dover, New Jersey.*

Le vierge, le vivace, et le bel aujourd'hui . . .

What were they like as schoolboys? Long on themes
And short of wind, perpetually outclassed,
Breaking their glasses, always chosen last
    When everyone was sorted out in teams,

Moody, a little dull, the kind that squirmed
At hurt cats, shrank from touching cracked-up birds,
With all but plain girls at a loss for words,
    Having to ask to have their fishhooks wormed,

Snuffers of candles every priest thought nice,
Quenchers of their own wicks, their eyes turned down
And smoldering. In Dover, my home town,
    No winter passed but we had swans in ice,

Birds of their quill: so beautiful, so dumb,
They'd let a window glaze about their feet,
Not seeing through their dreams till time to eat.
A fireman with a blowtorch had to come

Thaw the dopes loose. Sun-silvered, plumes aflap,
Weren't they grand, though?—not that you'd notice it,
Crawling along a ladder, getting bit,
Numb to the bone, enduring all their crap.

The Korean Emergency

Under Mount Etna's shadow, the Exec
In apoplexy on the quarterdeck
Razzing the OD,
                    Boy, for Chrissake clear
These guineas out of here,
                          our destroyer swung,
A broody sow hard set on by her shoats,
Bumboats,
The oiled tide
Swelling a moment only to subside,
Hesitant as breath from an injured lung.

All shat shaved shoeshined showered-off, each bore
His wait for boatspace, out for his own turn
To hit the beach with fifty bucks to burn.
Spilled out of floating nests their fathers poled,
Sharp-beaked bambinos in wrapped-rag shoes tore
Through GI cans for our potato peels,
Shivering. Although it didn't seem too cold.

We'd only to desire and they'd desire.
We rolled our stones, they gathered in our moss.
How not to admire
That one-eyed painter never at a loss
Given the dimmest wallet-snapshot? Lo,
Back came the spitting image of your girl
Staring in oils, ringed with a holy glow,
Eerie, some stranded pearl
Bloated a yard across.
A round red token like a meat-ration point
You gave the broad and, afterward, made whole,
Blessed with a pro kit from the Shore Patrol,
Tackled the guided tour of Syracuse,
Its Roman theater some crab's
Picked gutted shell. Let loose,
The lira leaking out of your dress blues,
You'd wander, up for grabs,
Through droves of boys who'd feel you up and pluck,
Or, if it were your will
Down on the beach or under some dark arch,
Nurse or give suck.

Who'd hate a thirst that held him in its sway
When the deep wine dish of the Mediterranean lay
Within his hands? Once more
We steamed back home. To meet us on the dock
Sat Gene's Dry Cleans.
                    Emergency, not war.

Girl Sketching Me into Her Landscape

Slim-fingered drudger, charcoal smudge on chin,
Sizing me up with quick strokes, am I in?
In your enchanted wood, whence none escape?
I'm flattered. OK, make off with my shape.
If I come back transfigured to a swine,
Who will declare the fault entirely mine?
From what I've seen tacked up, you can't draw water.
You plan on "going into art"? Oh, daughter,
What would you learn? How man bends at the knee?
Better bone up on such anatomy
At first hand: throw out chalk and measuring-string,
Set those light pendulums your wrists to swing;
On scaffoldings of gesture let you rise
Into the fixed frame of your lover's eyes.

For Time can't see straight. Let him, and he'll hew
Successive torsos more and more askew.
By months as by soft moths our fabric's rent
And ages eye us with obscene intent.
Quick! from the mold the good Lord gave you, cast
Your children, that a trace of you may last.

Skin will outlinger patinas of gold,
Bones bloom again though anapests grow old.
As if we'd had a child, we two endure
Each other's lines in mutual caricature,
But no we don't. Your hand swirls, there's a tree
Slammed like a door—and where's the likes of me?

Apocrypha

I

Still lay the world before He set man here.
On deeps He walked, a Sound without an ear,
Light without eye. On sleeping man He walked,
Out shot a spare rib and sat up and talked.

II

Great Yahweh fingered through His Bible,
Thought on it, and filed suit for libel.

III

Cain stuck a knife in Abel,
Threw the cold clay under the table,
And, having beheld his deed,
Had him a hearty feed.

What carcasses he did carve!
Ought not he have been let to starve
Who would spurn, for dry figs in Nod,
That groaning board of God?

Nothing in Heaven Functions as It Ought

Nothing in Heaven functions as it ought:
Peter's bifocals, blindly sat on, crack;
His gates lurch with the cackle of a cock,
Not turn with a hush of gold as Milton had thought;
Gangs of the slaughtered innocents keep huffing
The nimbus off the Venerable Bede
Like that of an old dandelion gone to seed;
And the beatific choir keep breaking up, coughing.

But Hell, sleek Hell hath no freewheeling part:
None takes his own sweet time, none quickens pace.
Ask anyone, How come you here, poor heart?—
And he will slot a quarter through his face,
You'll hear an instant click, a tear will start
Imprinted with an abstract of his case.

Creation Morning

Needing nothing, not lonely nor bored,
Why should He have let there be light?
We can only guess: a pool
Turns us so peaceful a face
That, unsettled, we take up a stone
To shatter that placidness.

Could it have been what boys know
At the rim of a new-laid sidewalk
That for empty blocks extends
Like the smooth crest of a moon
Until the tip of the chalk
Drags the hand in its wake?—

What he knows who beholds in his bride
Only her willingness,
He placing clothes on a chair,
She lying on one white side
With an imminent look?
That might have been how it was.

Who would not start growth rings
Breaking on shores of bark
At the toss of a seed like a stone,
Though not an eye look on
In that time nor in any time,
Though in the solid dark?

Space

for Martin Green

I

Who could have thought, but for eight days in space,
The heart might learn to thrive on weightlessness,
As though with no flesh holding it in place,
Yearning by choice, not made to by distress,
Turning in free fall on reprieve from earth
We tug-of-war with daily for the sakes
Of those we long for, those we help bring forth.
How will it be when all the strength it takes
To rip moons loose from planet boughs, or send
Engines of slag careening from their track
Into the unending dark, end over slow end,
Is in the twist that opens a door a crack?
Who will need long to savor his desire
When wishes no more blunt them against bulk,
But pierce straight through; when acts, once dreamt, transpire?
Man may imagine man's own mother's milk.

II

Heads bowed in fetal crouch, the Gemini
Float in their pear-shaped comfort. Data grows
By little clicks, as pine cones, drying free
And dropping, pile up. Enter, through a hose,
Essence of roast beef. Signs that flash ABORT
Bespeak a tube's break. If all hold, instead,
The moon's thin skin shall cringe under their boots—
Just as we always thought, the thing's stone dead.

III

Hope to be disembodied reconciles
Our drifted hearts to that exacting beat.
We clerks-without-church look on while slide-rules
Render our lusts and madnesses concrete.
It may well be that when I rev my car
And let it overtake and pass my thinking,
It's space I crave; when my electric bar
Sets up a moonshot, lemon-oiled and clinking,
And gulp by gulp, I shrug the world's dull weight,
Out after what I had long thought I'd hate.

Reading Trip

> Everybody's in po biz.
> *Louis Simpson*

Just past a grove where roots in overthrow
  Work air for nothing and boughs lie, still clung
With oranges stopped short, the towers show,
  Slim exhalations from a plastic lung,
    Shimmering distinctly: knowledge reared with pride.
    Whose Hell is here? Nutt's letter for my guide,

I ask the straight way to the English Dep't
  Of girls too beautiful ever to be of use,
Wondering by what husbandry they're kept
  Golden and huge, aburst with squeezing juice.
    The secretary, withered on her bough,
    Unclicks a gate latch: "Mister Nutt's yours now."

A handshake, hearty, fingers a little stiff
  (From years of etching grades on freshmanese?),
A pool-cue-following eye, though. Kind as if
  I'd been John Clare, or one of the Trustees.
    Miss Cone will Beatrice me to the hall.
    God bless Nutt, there'll be liquor after all.

With buzzer Nutt invokes his teaching bard
  Whose class has just let out: who gropes at length
For the right gambit, picking his key word.
  He's read me, I've read him. Testing his strength,
    Each circles each, protecting his behind,
    Not knowing, sniffing after his own kind.

I'm in his hands for—what? A temperance lunch
  With all our eyebeams stuck fast to our plates?
With namecards, with the Tuesday-Thursday bunch
  Mulling the phases of the moon of Yeats?
    Jerusalem set free! he knows a bar
    For hot corned beef! "Come on, I've got a car."

And there in the click and hush of shuffleboard,
  Bridging our distances with pitcher-beer,
Something not far from sour truth being poured,
  Each makes out what the other has to bear.
    Close as a brace of long-lost concubines,
    We drink up, and misquote each other's lines.

After I'm let to stop off at the john,
  It's time to do my poet act, the house
A thin fourth filled and looking put upon,
   Except for one attentive-as-a-mouse
      Pale braided lass with twitching button nose.
      Nutt rallies all to man the front-line rows.

I offer Hardy's "Ruined Maid," on watch
  For hints of acquiescence. About half
Coolly endure, let out their yawns a notch;
   Some look about—are they supposed to laugh?
      But here and there, a grin, unprepossessed,
      Shimmers, a lump of ore that's passed its test.

And after, the popcorn-burst of handclaps spent,
  Will some hang on? Why, sure as Hell, released,
A few struggle forward, bold or hesitant,
   The better to read the fine print on the beast.
      Pale Mouse steals up on tiptoe and I'm slipped
      A morsel of her own mauve manuscript.

"How do you get ideas to write about?"—
  I fumble for the old stuffed-owl replies:
"Oh I don't know, I guess I just start out
   With a few words that match." "What market buys
      Ballads on water sports?"—my shoulders sag.
      "Don't you find riming everything a drag?"

A drag, man? Worse than that! Between the eyes,
  I take the blade of his outrageous stare.
Whoever crosses him, the varlet dies,
    Trapped Guest to his unancient Mariner:
      "Get with it, baby, what you want to be
      So artsy-craftsy for? Screw prosody,

"Turn it on, man, it's like for now, today,
  Disposable stuff, word-Kleenex. Why take pains
Trimming it neat? Nobody gonna play
    That game no more." A man worth crossing brains
      And tanking up with, wrestling with all night—
      But not tonight, man. Let me off tonight.

The bard reprieves me. Soon there's clinking ice
  And bourbon in suburbia, a haze
Of settled evening. Out of artifice,
    Sated with me and all my works and days,
      I guess what drove one Welsh bard wild to squeeze
      Buttock and bottle. Miss Cone cuts blue cheese.

And here, in this kindly orchard of the blest,
  Whose pretext for a stiff drink I have been,
This tenured, literate Oktoberfest
    That even paid to let me make its scene,
      Earth, it appears, will be bare earth indeed
      When they're chopped down, the last ones left who'll read.

Recloistered in the dry cell of my car,
  Ego discharging back to natural size,
I grope for balance, break off and discard
  Like petals of artichoke, the lies
    I stick out with all over, fumbling for
    A means to shrivel back to some sort of core,

Edge out into the dusk to claim my slot
  In the home-droning traffic, less and less
The bard on fire, more one now with the blot
  That hoods the stars above Los Angeles,
    Hard gunning, on the make for far-off nights,
    Like any other pair of downcast brights.

October

How high they'd rear,
Those gold-leaf hills I'd take
Crash landings into,
Throwing away the hard work I had been to.

I scrape with care.
What ratshit clogs my rake.

West Somerville, Mass.

I

DAY 7

Sundays we wake to tumbrils: iron wheels
Crack pebbles as they mount through Somerville's
Evasive sunshine. Round our blinded room,
From wall to wall reverberations drum:
Our newsboy with his railway baggage cart
Toils Medford Hill, up past the bleeding heart
Of the doll stuck in Apicelli's lawn,
Bearing the fat white body of the *Globe*
That comes in sections like a sacred robe,
Swearing as though he had it in for dawn.

The boy's breath coarsens, torn forth from his ribs.
They're sitting up now, crowing in their cribs,
Throwing things. I quit my dozing wife,
Fumble tied shoestrings—O Lord, for a knife!—
Raise broken blinds, let daylight trickle through.
What was it, once, I used to have to do?

This day means beef not ground, and unmade dollar,
This day means Mutt and Jeff will come in color,
Time to feed tame ducks stale crusts, freed from pressure
As shaving cream sprung from its can. Let's raze.
Deep in the mirror I confront two eyes
Like the last windowpanes you'd see in blocks
Doomed to renewal, so far spared boys' rocks.

II

THE ASCENT

The rock rolled back, the stained race hatched out new,
They pass my window, the communicants,
Each with two neat knife-edges in his pants.
In bathrobe still, out of it as a Jew,

Wonder Bread toast, cold coffee at my teeth,
I mark time on a half-baked villanelle
That will not rise. Lord knows, up Medford Hill
I'd go, but stop short before that wraith

My body risen, back, the old hale fellow,
All the same hangnails, chilblains, the whole bit,
Arms out for soul to re-embrace with it.
He'd be hard tack to swallow,

And, feet fast rotting, how to toe the line
On Mary's hoist to Heaven? Call it myth,
But that's pale stuff to slake a body with,
Water after Pope John's wine.

My faith copped out. Who was it pulled that heist?
Wasn't it me, too stuck-up and aloof
To spill my sins? If knocked on for a roof,
I wouldn't have a chair to offer Christ,

But He'd no more halt at my door than they,
Unless to frown in on my snotty kids
Aping their bonnets, sporting potty lids.
One dark duenna screws up lips to slay

Me with a word. Peace, Momma!—I'd go back
To forehead ashes, giving up for Lent,
But I gave up every blessed sacrament.
Can the strait gate still stand open a crack?

Who'd grudge joy to an angel, if it can?
Last night in the bathtub, groping for the soap,
I tried a sloppy act of love, felt hope
Drum at my heart with vague feet. Pregnant man,

What's eating you? Good Friday, on to plunge
His lance, a soldier stepped in, drove up hard,
Laughed and drew back. The captain of the guard
Offered a vinegar-soaked sponge.

Again, eventual as spring, some goodman begs
The Body, decks it out in his own tomb,
Limbs in clean linen, wounds touched with sweet balm.
It took place while I shopped for Easter eggs.

O lukewarm spew, you, stir yourself and boil
Or be not chosen. Strike with your whole weight
At hook, line, sinker—be fished, or cut bait—
Give, or get off the pot—

My boy steps up. He bites the loosening ear
Of his milk-chocolate rabbit. Limb from limb
The victim's rendered. Let us eat of him
Some other year.

Each dawn the children rout me out. What profit
To shrink back like a dumb bulb? At a loss,
I stretch out arms, fix feet as on a cross
Till something says, *Come off it.*

III

GOLGOTHA

Gray fur collars on a steel limb,
The welders, keeping hands warm
Inside their sheet-plastic cocoon,
Weave the new dorm

Late into night, deadlined
For April. According to plan,
The chewed hill's to be redefined
And seedlings, to a man,
Stood up in ranks to face blight,
Green lawn unrolled,
Brick walls, adolescently bright,
Sprayed to look old.

In my locked childproof basement work room,
Furnace vapors
Chase their own tails. Roof-high, loom
Ungraded papers.
An iron door in a brick wall
A kick could splinter
Dikes back the ashes of all
Our hearths of winter.
I half-hear the thrash of bed sheets,
A mouse scratch, taking chances.
Down the spine of my dogeared John Keats
Mildew advances.

Cramped handwriting, don't know his name:
"How Youth Is Shafted
By Society"—now I've pegged him,
They got him. Drafted.
(Through vines in a gnarled neutral zone,
A locust nation,
Flamethrowers grazing, moves on
About its task, defoliation.)

Interesting idea, says my pen
To a John Bircher—liar, liar!—
Shots rattle. No, the stuffed lion's
Brass eyeballs in the dryer.

I take out trash, not to read more—
Torn gift wraps, Christmas-tree rain—
Lift can-cover on a white horde
Writhing. Lean rain
Blown to bits by the murderous wind
Has it in for you, finger and face,
Drives through every hole to your brain,
Taking over the place
As though it had been here before,
Had come back in its own hour,
Snow gaining ground in the dark yard,
The mad in absolute power.

II
Countrymen

Main Road West

The Late Show, on the rebound from the hill
Propping the Oak Motel, gives up its ghost:
A star who's lain dead longer than she'll tell
Undergoes face-lifts . . . loses voice . . . is lost . . .
The channel slithers from the set's blunt hook.
No magazines, no book but the Good Book.

Half-parted drapes, snapped lock, and a long drink
In a glass meant for water. Almost gone,
Trees that have leaves, as though you'd crossed a brink.
The wind's turned off; the sign USED CARS, still on
That keeps hard stars from piercing through to town,
As though stars will be foresworn, or stared down.

Requiem in Hoboken

Their wives and children, spiffed up fit to kill,
Take front seats for the breaking of the crust,
Choir hums the Miserere, china saints
From Barclay Street ask, squint-eyed, what they'd cost;
The celebrant, among chrysanthemums
Brought just a wink before the Bird with bread
(Whistled straight off our Heavenly Father's fist)
Had made delivery (ward-heelers gave most),
Moves threshingly in black to twist the Host,
Taste the raised wine. Peace drop upon these men
Of Hoboken the 5:11 train
Suddenly cut to lengths befitting dust.

How can the grandest resurrection ever
Cover their patchwork shells and, one by one,
Warm up the nestful till they hatch to Heaven
Without their thirsting at the very throne
For Guinness's (two free rounds out of seven)?
Though graves give in, tired wharves weight's overgrown,
Christ, if you've got no hardboiled eggs to crack
On your marble bar, they'll bitch to be stuck back.

The Bird broods on a setting of brown stone.

O'Riley's Late-bloomed Little Son

O'Riley's late-bloomed little son,
Shown off for seven weeks,
Frostbitten, shrank back in again.
They'd picked him up to find out if
His croup would stop, them holding him,
But in their arms he just went stiff.

They say she's past her change of life.
You'll see them Saturdays
In the back yard, her breaking ground
For a white birch, him on a mound
No higher than that where their hope lies,
Reaching, cold beer in other hand,
For Lucille and Camille's pop flies.

For a Flung Cyclist

With revolutionary eye,
   The watching squad car clears you space
   To drop out of the human race
On the cracked asphalt where you lie

Tired of a speed that grew like mad,
   Black helmet busted where the pole
   You didn't see got through your skull
Like no advice you ever had.

The Strip lifts one nine-mile-long voice
   To moan you. What wheel have you left.
   A stretcher hands your bones a lift
To make way for a white Rolls-Royce.

Your star's turned to a paving stone.
   Confused and true to it you died,
   Unlike those of us who have lied
And not so soon are overthrown.

Down in Dallas

Down in Dallas, down in Dallas
Where the shadow of blood lies black,
Little Oswald nailed Jack Kennedy up
With the nail of a rifle crack.

The big bright Cadillacs stomped on their brakes,
The street fell unearthly still
While, smoke on its chin, that slithering gun
Coiled back from its window sill.

In a white chrome room on a table top
They tried all a scalpel knows,
But they couldn't spell stop to that drop-by-drop
Till it bloomed to a rigid rose.

Out on the altar, out on the altar
Christ blossoms in bread and wine,
But each asphalt stone where his blood dropped down
Is burst to a cactus spine.

Oh down in Dallas, down in Dallas
Where a desert wind walks by night,
He stood and they bound him foot and hand
To the cross of a rifle sight.

Among Stool Pigeons

I

Falling between two stools, his forehead cracked
   Hard on the finger-painters' bench. The sums
Like hay caught in a hurricane came unstacked.
   From head to foot he felt himself all thumbs.

Oddly enough, the lesson plan went on.
   Brim-full of gin, he watched the ceiling: wheels
Skipped from their axle. Sprawled in a cold stun,
   Expecting Miss Runcible's smart peck of heels,

Foresaw the Board meet, beetle-browed: *"The rap
   Is moral turp, twerp—what you got to say?"*
"Fongoo."
       "Guards! Seize him!"
                  "Catch me!"
                        End your yawp
   And come away,

You hoot-owl treading snow,
    Quit. When the weight of that soaked hulk you are
Breaks through the crust, you might as well let go.
    This stuff's for wrens to tiptoe on. The car

Has one more payment due—rouse! Christ, I'm crocked,
    Old head's all puddles . . . Glenda had to go . . .
Here comes that star-splashed dark . . . Was I half-cocked
    To give the pigeons *Opium* by Cocteau?

II

Upon his mouth the children, twittering, wove
    A second mouth before they stole away
To tell on him and kindly pressed it there:
    Corners turned down, light blue, of modeling clay.

For a Maiden Lady

A tremor in her wrist
Forbade us to exist.
Fevers arose to burn
Her few twigs. All concern
Run past, her look congealed
Like a spare boudoir sealed
Against the gilt snuff box,
Lavengro, the lace clocks
She had crocheted when able,
The postcard on the table,
Chrysanthemums still damp,
The stopped moth by the lamp,
And we who had played kind,
So much dust thrust from mind.

Cities

Old as a rind of moon, half cracked they are,
Bleary-eyed, better looking in a bar,
Pale as if sick, each smelling like a nurse,
A sawed-off shotgun in her beaded purse.

Scholar's Wife

All winter long, your book *The Doric Mood*
Advanced while I lay sleeping in the nude
Or reading, sucking caramels, on my back.
I'd hear downstairs your typewriter attack
The barricades of learning till, the skin
Of suburbs pierced, your column spurted in.
Shivering, I'd draw the bedclothes tight against my chin.

The long nights wane. Judicious notes lie bare.
How can I miss what never has been there?
The dying God with rose thorns through his hands
Has given no sign that he understands.
Who else is there to talk to? So I write
This daily journal. Not mine to indict,
The new-mown snow soft toppling down in stacks.
I clutch my ballpoint. Lick it. To relax
The pelvic girdle I take endless baths,
Go to confession: *See five Day of Wraths*
And ten Potemkins. Promise to amend
Your life. Drink less, avoid your husband's friend.

Why suffer me—or on me? Don't come back
Unless for who I am, not for some pack
You rip the tab from, give a flick, unzip,
Puff and crush out. Your sexual Reddi-dip.
But oh, I'm hard on you. For you've embraced
Me always in your thought, you said, and placed
Beside my bed to keep watch on me, pet,
This Japanese miniature television set.

Pottery Class

On Wednesday nights, the children rinsed and stacked,
The wives, their husbands closeted with *Time*,
From Lexington and Concord motor in
To travail in the elemental slime.

Thwack! and a hunk of muck hung by the heels
Has its back slapped, its breathing made to come.
Vast casseroles take shape on groaning wheels,
A vase commences like all Christendom.

Darlings, what's eating you? What is it drives
Your sleepless hands to take up earth to knit?
Dull flickswitch chores? The drag of being wives?
The void a child leaves open after it?

Lay your manicures waste, dears, though you may,
Yours is the furious core man stands outside
Gazing on, helpless, while you shape his clay
And blast him till he's dried.

The Self-exposed

On the Bangor-bound platform, the crowd became one
Shaping lips to me: *Now, sweet, now!*—
On the handle of my zipper, my hand dragged down,
Out it budded, my golden bough

In that plate-glass proscenium my Pullman room.
An old biddy guffawed, a valise
Being handed up to a conductor's hand
Blossomed underwear, a man yelled *Police!*—

Then we lurched, I was gone. What gets into me?
I'm not one to be peter-proud,
But my bird-out-of-hand longs to take its stand
On the farther side from what's allowed.

People with their foreheads like income tax forms
Raise the puke in me! How I yearn
To scribble with the dibble on their neat-ruled norms.
They'll nail me yet. I never learn.

Oh, I've been to psychiatrist and priest,
I've read an uplifting book,
But it's cold, and I hunger to walk forth dressed
In the quilt of the world's warm look.

Absentminded Bartender

He'd meant to scare her, just, not hurt,
Who would have thought so light a tap . . . ?
Hey, you asleep?
     He gave a start,
Cut off head dribbling from the tap.

Cities and hotels
Since then had made one corridor
Of bulbs, extinguishers. Somewhere else
Was where he hung out more and more,
And drinking, though it made days worse,
Blurred how it had been, looking back,
And made time harder to reverse
Unless he had an egg to crack
And burst the yolk of.
     In his room,
Sunlight locked out, there sought for ease
In fresh positions legs and arms
Severed, alive, in bed with his.

National Shrine

Sanctioned by eagles, this house. Here they'd met,
Undone their swordbelts, smoked awhile and posed
Gazes that could not triumph or forget,
And held their jowls set till a shutter closed.

Kentucky rifle now, and Parrot gun
Cohabit under glass. Connecticut
And Alabama, waxed sleek in the sun,
Reflect like sisters in the parking lot.

Lee's troops led home to gutted field and farm
Mules barely stumbling. Borne off in each car,
The wounded sun and instant Kodachrome
Render our truces brighter than they are.

The Old

Mushrooms, their deafnesses
Feed on their heads and sprout
In circles round them. Restlessly
They pace their rest homes, wens and welts
On their hands, snatching obituaries:
They live for death's evening race results.

Bowed down, they set out late from home
To Leisure Worlds and Seniorvilles
Where, ill behind green gravel lawns
And rubber shrubs, the sun going down
Trips an electric gate, expels
The final child from town.

Bring dominoes and biscuits, all
You heirs they're flesh to. Let them lack
Nothing they'll need to have a ball.
Bring instant splints in case shins crack;
For picture windows, if they can crawl,
The placard HELP ME—HEART ATTACK.

Best Seller

The copy we'd sent off for, on its rounds
Growing dog-eared, the pack of us in there
Saw ourselves whipped and, smarting from our wounds,
Took to our legs and bayed. In Courthouse Square
Faster and faster till the dustclouds spun
Our spastic schoolbus driver gunned his bus
On finding out that he had put him in
And made him out the one whole man of us.

So mad we hitched a scarecrow to a limb,
Set it on fire and tore its britches down,
We could light on no names too low for him—
That is, until the guided tours hit town,
Bought two-bit tickets to the chickencoop
Old Wylie'd rigged to pass off for the scene
Of the big gang-bang, ate our tall tales up
And guzzled us bone-dry of gasoline.

Well. This was different. So we nailed up boards
To show where he'd been born and had lived last,
Rooted a stunty peach tree in the yard
Where Elfa's baby fires the shotgun blast

That unmans its own father, passed the hat
And set a granite skullcap on the head
Of Scholar Alpaugh's statue—did all that
To put things more in line with how he'd said.

We might have known. The nameplate of the town
High on the depot wall has flaked so dim
You have to squint at it. We'd take it down
And paint it fresh, but, on account of him,
We're written up in guidebooks now, and, stuck,
We ghost about the daylight feeling thin,
Like stolen bones that ought to be put back.
Only one train, now, bothers with our track.

Hot nights, sleep holding off, in the one bar,
Called Elfa's Nest, chairs propped up to the wall,
Watching the ash of Horace Coe's cigar
Hang on like one last rubberneck's eyeball,
We don't talk much. The whole town's on a shelf,
Thick under webs no hand's about to muss.
Just the wind making echoes to itself,
The wind, the parched wind goes on fingering us.

Loose Woman

Someone who well knew how she'd toss her chin
   Passing the firehouse oglers, at their taunt,
   Let it be flung up higher than she'd want,
Just held fast by a little hinge of skin.
Two boys come from the river kicked a thatch
   Of underbrush and stopped. One wrecked a pair
   Of sneakers blundering into her hair
And that day made a different sort of catch.

Her next-best talent, setting tongues to buzz,
   Lasts longer than her best. It still occurs
   To wonder had she been our fault or hers
And had she loved him. Who the bastard was,
Though long they asked and notebooked round about
   And turned up not a few who would have known
   That white inch where her neck met shoulderbone,
Was one thing more we never did find out.

What She Told the Sheriff

Hot nights out in the cornshocks,
    Snakelike they'd go
Bashing about in pickup trucks,
    Headlights on low,
Staking out soft beds in Hell,
    Giggling. Till morning,
Safe on my windowsill,
    I'd do the darning,
Three-way lamp all the way up,
    Hymns turned on louder,
Knees tight locked, china cup
    Of headache powder
Running over. I'd kiss Christ
    (My own right arm)
Or read till, my eyes crossed,
    Red words would squirm.
I'd pray: Change places, Lord,
    Stroke by stroke the corn
Watches You nailed back on Your board
    Sure as You're born.

Lend me the power to damn
    Those lipsticked, caving
Doors to man's battering-ram.
    What one's worth saving?—
No sign. Only the moon's gleam,
    Monotonous tick talk
From the wall clock, shine of ice cream
    Bowls from the dish rack,
Four years locked in a frame
    Instead of marriage:
The sheepskin bearing my name
    Like some miscarriage.
Paul said, *Our days in earth*
    Are as a shadow . . .
Father no doubt slept with
    His plump grass-widow
While Mother courted sleep,
    As ever ailing,
Spending life's ocean trip
    Hugged to the railing.
Next noon, out choosing ears
    For the lunch pot,
I'd come on sin's arrears
    Still body-hot:
There in the scrambled dirt
    The telltale pressings
Of buttocks, a torn-off shirt,
    Love's smelly passings.
Father, how could Your Hand
    Deign to forgive?

Smite them! Don't understand,
　　Don't just let live!
I'd weep, the sun's broadsword
　　Carving my bonnet,
For this blood-handed world
　　And all here on it.
Then one noon, my Maker's ways
　　Laid themselves bare.
Scabs fell down from my eyes,
　　All stood forth clear:
Worms, worms in leaf and ear,
　　Kernel and tassel,
Gnawing the Wurlitzer
　　In Burger Castle!
Hell peered through surgeon's slits,
　　Burst out of faucets—
Babies chopped off at the root,
　　Crushed flat in corsets!
My heart caught fire in me,
　　Fire hard to cover—
How endlessly time marks time
　　When God's your lover—
And it was all I could do
　　Till my right hour
To hold a lid over my glow,
　　Sifting cake flour.
Midnight. Led by my sword,
　　Ripe for reborning,
I strode in where Dad snored,
　　Mother lay turning:

Two old and swollen sheep
    Stretched out for slaughter,
Teeth set adrift to keep
    In mineral water,
They were like chopping wood.
    Drunk, uncomplaining,
And wondering Dad stood
    A long while draining.
Mother half raised her, coughed,
    Said—for once painless—
Girl, wipe that cleaver off,
    That one's not stainless.
Next, blazing kerosene
    Wiped the brown oily
Head-shaped time-honored stain
    From Dad's chair doily.
Along the henhouse path,
    Dry faggots crackled.
At each step I shook earth with
    The bantam cackled.
Saint Michael goaded me,
    Grass fire his halo,
Render unto Your Father on high
    Your father's silo!
Wrath roared in my right hand,
    How soon it catched
Where, like deceivers' tents,
    Hay sat pitched.
Creatures of hoof and horn,
    Sheol's lumps of tallow,

Struck at walls of their barn
    That soon grew hollow.
Far as earth led the eye,
    Smoke bloomed, burnt stubble
Crawled legless. It was I
    Cast down the Devil.
Why did you handcuff me?
    Let go! By morning
All Iowa could be
    One high bush, burning.

Edgar's Story

What we'd been missing out on all those years
Of stoking up the coffeepot at dawn,
Those Sundays, sitting working on some beers,
Watching the sprinkler going on the lawn
Was what we wanted. Gassed the old tin can
And lit out up the turnpike, Nell and I,
Soon as I got my fourteen-karat pen
And pencil set, and wrote, and it went dry.

Woods were the good part: straight up, all their limbs
Creaking with leaves. But then we'd have to go
Gawk at some china plates and hand-carved looms.
Freight cars sat idling, sad towns in their tow
And snake farms where you stood and looked at snakes.
Now all those plastic squirrels that say, *I'm nuts*
For the Dakota Bad Lands on their butts,
That nobody laughs at, long, give me cold shakes.

Somehow out there with not much else around
In the motel at night, it starts to hurt,
Thinking, and your head beginning to pound
In time to the drip-drying of your shirt,

Of redwood forests melted down for pulp.
It ties a knot in my bowels
Every time I cost a branch to take a crap
And dry my hands off on some paper towels.

At Mount Rushmore I looked up into one
Of those faces born joined to the same neck bone.
I said, *Abe, Abe, how does it feel to be up there?—*
And that great rock he has for a pupil budged, I swear,
And he looked me in the eye and he said, *Alone.*

Peace and Plenty

Bound to the road by chains
Of motels, hills of pines
Under the moon lie stunned.
An Adirondack stirs
Winds, groping for her firs.
Engines are gunned

And, not knowing which path to choose
Through the chemical plant, the river
Choked with refuse
Upturns a blithering stare
To the exhausted air.
Crows hover.

Let the new fallen snow
Before she change her mind
Lay bare her body to the Presto-Blo,
The drooped rose her
Quietus find
Head down inside the in-sink waste-disposer.

Driving Cross-country

Jack Giantkiller took and struck
  His harp and stalks sat up, all ears—
With wavelengths corn in Keokuk
  Comes on so hard it interferes.

Glass vacant, in the Stoplight Lounge,
  Expecting to be stood a meal,
Ella Ashhauler has to scrounge,
  Her slipper tilted, for some heel.

Where is the prince of yesteryear
  Beneath whose lip princesses roused?
Bourbon will add a gleam of cheer.
  The place has lately been deloused.

Prints of a bowling-ball-eyed child
  Brood over ornamental pewter.
A wand's been waved, the whole house styled
  To offend no one, by computer:

A room the same as last night's room,
  Exact same bath mat underfoot.
In thrall to some unlucky charm,
  We hurtle; but, it seems, stay put.

When, headlight-blind, we let fall head
  On pillows hard by right-hand lanes
In airconditioned gingerbread,
  It keeps on driving through our veins,

Some hag's black broth. At dawn we stare,
  Locked into lane by rule of lime.
We had a home. It was somewhere.
  We were there once upon a time.

Vietnamese

I

FARMER

> There was small rice to spare,
> We had raised ample weeds, disease and pillage,
> Children of cheek
> Deep as the ditch we dug for them, though weak.
>
> Upon our village
> The fire fell, making sure.
>
> I would have fled.
> I was old, though, and poor.

II

HIRED PILOT

> Each thatched shack where old men had sat in thought
> I tore out of the village like a page.
> The air keeps quiet. Nothing will engage.

What matter who the quick are, who the dead?
The dead don't want, the living are well paid
If wise. And it is wisdom to be bought.

What am I? Scurf on the Great Buddha's head,
But not yet scratched. Not yet.
                              Fueled by a year
Of rice out of a peasant's gut, I hang
For a whole minute, whining, in midair.

The Medium Is the Message

Plugged in, stone deaf, sleepwalking into trains,
Teen-agers die, transistors at their brains,
Steps locked to rock, each mind a listening post,
At break of station giving up the ghost.
The rude beast slouches. Shall each child at birth
Be operated on and belted forth
With aerial built in and, his own screen,
Sit turned on, watching late shows in his bean?
Then, words in lines may be as obsolete
As hand-carved airplanes driven by steam heat.

Fresh beats the age insists on, not the heart's,
But those of rush-hour traffic's fits and starts.
Would I then drop out of my times? You bet!—
Could I but pack along my hi-fi set,
Electric light, a crate of books, canned beer
To help keep medieval ardor clear.
Then, hunched at my quill, I'd blow cold thumbs, perhaps,
Lest one word of Yeats lapse.

Ant Trap

Innocuous as a clock, giving off whiffs
Of roast beef, rare, and bathtubs full of gin
Free to the rank-and-file of working stiffs,
This Siren in a tin can lures them in.
A skull-and-crossbones on her lid warns men
Not to crack up against her reefs,
But how could that turn back an ant, his skin
Already bone, to whom death's head is life's?

Out through her punctured doors, down winding roads,
Each totes home his own and his kinsmen's doom
In trust. Recall those fourteen-year-old broads
Who'd stand across the street from Napoleon's Tomb,
Beckoning not with fingers but perfume
The tired GI in quest of other wars
And kinder arms than guns to come home from,
Remember how they stretched forth open pores.

Not that the gift he brought home was the clap,
Although he might have, no, nor just the can
Of Spanish fly our good Rotarian
Smuggled back home to storm his girl friend's lap,

No dirtybook nor head cut from a Jap
Scrubbed to a whitened skull in some latrine,
Nothing to shove a pin through on a map,
But wider than La Belle France's *belle poitrine*.

And now, kempt creature moving in straight files,
Social, in press, with jawbone razored sleek,
Hopping the shuttle daily, vaulting miles
To and from Scarsdale, hearing the same rails click,
Delivered nightly back to his Blest Isles,
Do his nerves go slack,
Does he sip with glazed eyes and frozen smile
His scotch-and-water in a state of shock,

Or find, perhaps, death ill disposed to come
And slow death a far cry from what he needs?
All that he'd hold they hold worth turning from,
His sons mock. Minds expanding, on mad creeds
Nurtured by moon in Katmandu, they bloom
Like vines that crack their temple steps; burn weed,
Smoke and explode his sunken livingroom
And, sooner than believe him, die from speed.

Then, too, the failure's failure: twitching, scared,
Half starved for more than fingers ever plucked.
In any bar you find him firmly chaired,
Gulping the day's war rumor, pissing fact,

His life one long decline from having warred
On others than himself. His hands extract
Invisible bayonets—he'd show the world,
Clean out the bastards. He and beer reflect.

By their soft weakening lights, you'd guess how all
That army shuttling through it in a train
With nothing but its sweetness on the brain
Must feel when, home, their pulsebeats falter and stall
And, clutching sides, they double up in pain,
Their footholds loosen, they begin to fall,
Reach forth slow feelers, grope, catch fast again,
Stiffening columns in behind a wall.

III
Growing into Love

Transparency

Love was the woman I loved,
A grave, inhuman woman.
At night in our room alone,
I, self-sufficient Adam,
Laid hand on my cold bone.

She could unhook her face
And, smiling, lay it down,
Pick up a living face
That wobbled in her hand
And smooth it on in place.

She'd turn to me dim lips
Held next my lips by will—
Yet, as we thinned to sleep,
Even through gorged eyes,
I could see through her skull.

Artificer

Blessing his handiwork, his drawbridge closed,
  He sabbathed on a hill of hand-tooled wax.
On stainless steel chrysanthemums there posed
  Little gold bees with twist-keys in their backs.

Nothing could budge in this his country: lewd
  Leaves could go slither other people's hills.
  His thrushes tried tin whistles in their bills;
His oaks bore pewter acorns that unscrewed.

Increase perfection! So, he shaped a wife,
  Pleated the fabric of her chartered thigh,
Begat sons by excisions of a knife
  In camphorwood. He warned them not to die.

The moment flowed. So did his cellophane
  Brook over rollers. All obdurate day
  His player-piano tunkled him its lay,
Though on its ivory dentures a profane

Tarnish kept ripening, and where high tide
　Slid on ballbearings ceaselessly to shore,
Red rust. All night, the world that lolled outside
　Kept slipping newborn rats under his door.

Ode

Old tumbril rolling with me till I die,
Divided face I'm hung with, hindside-to,
How can a peace be drawn between us, who
   Never see eye to eye?

Why, when it seems I speak straight from the heart
Most solemn thought, do you too have to speak,
Let out a horselaugh, whistle as I break
   The news to Mother that I must depart?

Moon always waxing full, barrage balloon,
Vesuvius upside down, dual rump roast,
Cave of the Winds, my Mississippi coast,
   Cyclops forever picking up and chucking stone,

Caboose, poor ass I'm saddled with from birth,
Without your act, the dirty deed I share,
How could the stuck-up spirit in me bear
   Coming back down to earth?

Hearthside Story

At seventeen, I spent cold cash
In Scranton on a piece of ash,
Two legs attached like logs of oak
Stacked for a burning. When she spoke
Came hiss and sputter; when she laughed,
A chimney with a faulty draft.
She snapped her Fleers, she punched which floor.
The DON'T DISTURB sign on our door,
A hot gust hurtled up my flue.
All night, the room a thickening blue,
What perfect ovals she could blow!
I watched the ashtrays overflow
While, on the andirons of the bed,
Two lipsticked clinkers in lips' stead
Purveyed me chips of frost on hire.
I had no heart to fan a fire
That chilled, I gave it up for good,
O Mistress mine, my kindling wood.

Wish

If only you were two of you,
   I'd save one for those nights
When, at the changing of the moon,
   You douse your loving lights,

And me, I'd be the Siamese Twins—
   Then, darling, all month long
I could get on with loving you
   Though fast asleep in Eng.

Mean Gnome Day

LOST MOTION: Looseness
which allows movement
between mating parts
supposed to turn in unison.
The Machinist Dictionary

The day comes limping in as though a hump
Stood on its back and bowed it. As we fall
Apart in bed, each to a separate lump,
We do not speak. Our thoughts are shrunk to dwarfs
Whose piggish eyeballs glitter as they curl
About to stroke their privates. In such weather
There is small remedy, no, none in gin.
Each could reach out, but neither will begin.
One takes a twisted measure of the other.

At supper even the pair of turkey pies,
Frozen, unpackaged, turn out deformed
As the white feet of a Chinese lady bound
In thongs to make them delicate and small.

Anyhow, we put them into the oven. Warmed,
They limp forth: thick, lopsided, overbrowned.
Eating with sidewise fork strokes, we sit bound
In self-drawn thongs, beholden to the wall.

Worn out at last from fixing lips so tight,
From propping up the bastions of our stares,
Something in us begins to yield towards night,
Even as though, inside a glacier,
His hand still fastened to his granite spear,
The matted form of some Neanderthal
Had been made out—blurred but alive—through swarms
Of frosted bubbles—chipped loose, boated south,
There to be thawed, there to bestir numb arms,
To try ripe fruit with unfamiliar mouth.

Two Apparitions

I

Half in dreams, half with me, she lay: some foal
  Hardly born. As I crossed her spine
With a hand, out to join it and bind her stole
  Another man's hand, not mine,

A scaled hand, a lizard's, blotched over with bile,
  Every knuckle a knot on a stick,
And in her cheek, dug there, a crone's wan smile.
  I shuddered. Wild-eyed she woke,

Then in the next moment, the moon's white rise
  Cast the two of us smooth once more
And we fell to each other with timid cries,
  Backs turned on what lay in store.

II

Where no man laid eyes,
Past our bedside wall
Slipped the head of the moon
Like a genital
Hardly able to rise,
Too cold to assuage
Having had to look on
In diseased old age.

Daughter in the House

This sleeping face, not even mine nor yours,
A hard thing to have charge of, not to own,
Settled on us through time, as ocean floors
Bestow them in long snowfalls made of bone:
A face half foreign, half of some we know,
Borne down upon her, as a gem occurs
Out of the first leaves ever tree let go,
From tons that crushed dead faces into hers.

Smooth as the skin laid on a pail of cream,
Her sleep hides ferment. Would we work her wrong
To lift it off and peer in on her dream?
Hasn't she been down in herself too long?
But no. Two pools abused by thunderbursts,
We regain balance in her quiet spells.
She is our drink. It was for her our thirsts
Singled out each other's wells.

Monday

The furred ears of the African violet
Listen to the sun. It tingles
Creeping over its own haired stems,
Over the droppings of the parakeet.
Kathleen is crying. Listen to the wind.

Coming down from the attic, the dressmaker's form
In my trivial arms, I leave you
To your steam-iron on the porch. The violet
Is blue, the flower for Monday and regret.

Giving In to You

Laird of my makeshift castle,
Drawbridge trussed up tight,
I sat in there without a light,
Hard striving to be facile

And wrote a book. It dried,
I stood it on my shelf
And fed, my pride
A mouth swallowing the body from around itself.

Shrill
As if a whistle-cord hung for my tail.
Given a pull,
I'd wail.

Ate bacon rind,
Bicarbonate; drank Diet-Rite root beer.
At night I'd double-lock and bar each ear.
Who'd mind?

Now I give in to you
As the house of the county poor's
Gauze curtains do
To the luxurious wind
That knows how to be kind,
That overflows all outdoors.

Lazy Plumbing

Letting the water run to get it hot,
I lay back down on my cot
And so did you.

A bobolink
Complained of the loss of water in the sink.

Morning grew hot.
Our coffeepot
Scorched through.

The Shorter View

Her eyes outstretched from seeing how in space
Stars in old age will stagger, drop, and burst,
Throwing out far their darknesses and dust,
My wife lets her book fall with stricken face.
She'd thought tomorrow set and rooted here,
And people. That some morning would occur
Without a sunrise hadn't dawned on her.
Kathleen some great pink shell held to her ear,
And, wistful, staring through me to an earth
Littered with ashes, too dried-up to bear—
Though I say, What the Hell, we won't be there—
She doesn't see much point in giving birth
And, in our dark bed where her burden grew,
When I'd make love and recklessly let live,
Her arms drawn shut, for this night will not give
One inch of ground for any shorter view.